TEEN GIRL'S SURVIVAL GUIDE

How to Make Friends, Build Confidence, Avoid Peer Pressure, Overcome Challenges, Prepare for Your Future, and Just About Everything in Between

By
Jenn Higgins

ISBN: 978-1-957590-28-8

For questions, email: Support@AwesomeReads.org

Please consider writing a review!

Just visit: AwesomeReads.org/review

FREE BONUS

SCAN TO GET OUR NEXT
BOOK FOR FREE!

TABLE OF CONTENTS

INTRODUCTION

You've obviously gotten your hands on this book, so that likely means that you're either already a teenager or about to enter into the wonderful world of your teens. Let us be the first to say congratulations! You made it, and you're about to enter some of the most exciting years of your life. You'll finally be able to watch some of those PG-13 movies you've been dreaming about, and once you learn to drive a car, you'll finally have the freedom to take yourself to the mall. Even after embracing full adulthood when you reach 18, you'll continue to make long-lasting relationships and learn to become the absolutely amazing woman you were meant to be.

However, although we would like to tell you otherwise, it won't all be sunshine, sparkles, and rainbows. Heck, there will be days where there is no sparkle at all. While we'd like to say that this is going to be an easy, breezy time for you, we aren't going to lie: These years will be full of change, and you'll have to learn how to function as a budding adult woman. This means dealing with acne; discovering how to eat a healthy, balanced diet; navigating the many changes that go along with puberty; and figuring out how to say no to peer pressure; among other new experiences. So, how will you survive all these changes? With this book, of course!

From developing the best workout routine for growing bodies to discovering how to craft the perfect makeup routine, you'll learn how to take care of your body the right way so that you can avoid unnecessary armpit stink and other body odors. That's right—body odors in the plural. Did you know there's more than one kind?

And maybe up until now, you have had a few awesome girlfriends (or guy friends) who have done everything with you. But as you enter your teenager years, you might start to notice boys for the first time in a way that you hadn't before. How do you deal with that? How do you even talk to boys? And what do you do when one talks to you?

There's no need to run and hide because we've got you covered with some of the best tips and tricks for navigating the inevitable boy crazies.

It sounds like a lot, doesn't it? Well, that's because *it is* a lot, and while some of the changes will come as expected, others might show up when you least expect. With this book, you'll learn how to deal with the challenges of your teens and be prepared for everything that life is about to throw at you. That said, read on and become a master of your teenage years with this comprehensive survival guide for teenage girls.

CHAPTER 1:

GET UP AND GET ACTIVE: CREATING THE ULTIMATE WORKOUT ROUTINE

You go to school and sit at a desk all day and then you go home and sit on the couch for the rest of the night, eating chips and scarfing down everything in sight. While this sounds relaxing, this sedentary lifestyle isn't healthy for your body. Instead, it's incredibly important to get up and get active so that you can maintain a healthy body weight and start to develop a routine for a healthy lifestyle.

In fact, the next few years are going to be incredibly important in developing healthy routines and habits that you will likely carry for the rest of your life. Plus, working out doesn't have to be boring. You can make it super fun by changing up your workout routine or trying to get your friends to work out with you. In this section, we will go over how to create the ultimate workout plan to stay in shape and keep your body fit and healthy.

Why Should I Work Out?

The reasons to work out are, honestly, endless. Not only will you feel better mentally, but your body will stay strong, and you'll feel so much healthier than if you maintained the "slouch potato" lifestyle and just hung out on the couch all the time. If you commit to exercising regularly, you can prevent weight gain, high blood pressure, abnormal levels of cholesterol, and overall poor lifestyle habits that can lead to bad health in later life. While some of these conditions don't really pertain to you now, your body in 20 to 30 years will thank you (we promise)!

In your head, you may be thinking that working out will help you get that perfect body and maybe even that influencer status. However, working out should become part of your routine for more reasons than a hefty Instagram or Tik Tok following (and we will go over the dangerous truth about social media in later sections, so hold tight!). For example, exercising can help boost your energy levels so that you feel energized and ready to take on any challenges that come your way. Additionally, working out releases endorphins in your brain that make you feel happy, optimistic, and enthusiastic. When your brain chemistry is happy, you're likely to feel less stressed and better able to manage anxiety and depression. Your teenage years will be stressful, so any help you can get with stress management is absolutely worth it!

Not only will you feel good, but working out will improve your self-image and self-esteem. Ongoing workout routines also increase your muscle strength, release tension in your body, improve blood circulation, and can even prevent bone loss. Truly, there are so many benefits to engaging in regular exercise. So, why not try to create the perfect workout plan?

Workout Plans for Teenage Girls

To create the perfect workout plan, you first need to understand exactly how much exercise you should be getting each day and week. Typically, teenage girls need about 60 minutes of moderate to vigorous activity on most days of the week. You should get about 300 minutes, or 5 hours, per week of moderate-intensity activity, or you can do 150 minutes of *vigorous* activity each week. While it's better to do both moderate and vigorous activities, you should choose a workout plan that feels good for your body.

For example, you could work out every day during the week and take your weekends off, or give yourself some extra time during the week for homework and then work out on weekends. Quite honestly, creating the perfect workout plan depends on your schedule and your preferences, so a lot of this is deciding what works best for you.

Some of the best physical activities to put into your workout plan should include cardio, muscle strengthening, and bone-strengthening exercises. While these may sound a little intimidating, you probably already know most of these exercises. You should also do a mix of moderate and vigorous exercise. When you are doing a moderate aerobic activity, you should still be able to hold a conversation with your friend. So, these types of activities are fantastic for spending time with your workout buddy. During vigorous activity, you shouldn't be able to say more than a few words to your partner before having to pause for a breath because you are working so hard.

Muscle-strengthening activities usually include some sort of resistance training, such as lifting weights or other heavy objects, like those giant tires that you see CrossFit people lifting. Bone-strengthening activities, on the other hand, include any exercise in which your body comes in contact with the ground. This contact is good for your body because it pushes force on the bones and promotes bone strength and growth.

Vigorous - Intensity

Bicycle riding

Jumping rope

Martial arts

Running

Tennis

Aerobics

Muscle - Strengthening

Sit-ups

Resistance exercise using body weight or resistance bands

Swinging on playground equipment/bars

Push-ups

Climbing wall

Cross-country skiing

Bone - Strengthening

Hopping

Basketball

Gymnastics

Skipping

Volleyball

Running

Additionally, there are so many types of exercises and ways to strengthen your body that finding an activity that is not only good for you but also fun and exciting doesn't have to be hard. In fact, you should throw several types of activities into your workout routine in order to exercise your body in different ways. If you stick to the same type of workout, your body might become too used to that particular exercise, and it may not be as rigorous as it was before. That's not to say that you won't get fitter or that your body will become more accustomed to exercise, but it's good to vary your workout routine. If you need any help finding an activity that sounds like it might fit into your exercise routine, check out the suggestions above.

Busting Myths About Building Muscle

Truth time. Girls will not completely bulk up if they work out with heavy weights. You heard me: You can lift heavy weights and not bulk up to the size of a heavyweight bodybuilder (unless you want to, and in that case, you'll want to seriously increase your protein and caloric intake!). In fact, lifting heavy weights is only going to make you stronger and tone your body. You can do weights workouts to improve the muscle tone of your arms, legs, abs, back, and more.

When planning a muscle-strengthening activity, you can choose to lift weights or focus on simple body-weight exercises. Or even better, you can do a combination of both. You should never disregard the power of a simple push-up and sit-up because these are both excellent exercises to tone your body.

There are three terms that you should become familiar with if you decide to add muscle strengthening to your workout routine: **intensity, frequency,** and **repetitions.**

- **Intensity** is how much weight or force you can lift. For instance, you may do bicep curls with 10-pound weights where the 10-pound weights are your intensity.
- **Frequency** is how often you do a given muscle-strengthening activity, such as doing leg day twice a week.
- **Repetitions** are how many times you lift a weight. If you do 20 push-ups, 20 is your number of repetitions.

There are many different muscle groups that you should work out when engaging in strength training. For example, you can work out your back with pull-ups and deadlifts, work your chest with bench presses and push-ups, or work your glutes with the classic squat. Keep in mind that many workouts will target several muscle groups at once, so you can easily work out entire muscle groups with just a few key movements.

If you're a beginner, you should try between three and five exercises per muscle group and only do between three and six sets of each. Make sure you also start with lighter weights as you begin training. Add weight as you grow stronger. Your body will let you know when you're ready!

How to Make Working Out More Fun

One of the biggest challenges with working out is that working out itself is not easy. In fact, when you start working out, you might feel like your lungs are going to burst and your muscles are just going to give out on you. Don't fret; this only lasts for a little bit, and once you get into a routine, it gets easier. Even so, you're probably wondering how you can make working out more fun so that you stay motivated to do it.

Work Out with a Friend

One of the best ways to stay motivated to work out is to have a buddy who will keep you accountable. Maybe you have a friend who also wants to start working out, or maybe you even have a friend who already does work out and you want to figure out how the heck she does it. Either way, finding a workout buddy is a great way to maintain your exercise routine.

Not only can your friend keep you company while you do that 20-minute jog, but they can also motivate you to try that next repetition or increase your weight to see if you are ready to up your intensity. Your friend can be your biggest ally, and you can both motivate each other to continue to do better and stay fit.

However, working out with a friend isn't for everyone. If you are a person who prefers to put on her headphones and go for a solo bike ride to clear her head, absolutely go for it.

There is nothing wrong with wanting to work out by yourself and challenge yourself that way. You do you, girl!

Change Up Your Routine

If you do the same workout over and over again, you might find that it gets a little old. When the workout gets old, you might not be as motivated to continue, and your workout routine might lapse. Instead of waiting to get bored of your routine, plan to change up your schedule.

On Mondays, maybe you go for a jog and do a series of push-ups, but on Wednesdays, you focus on yoga and flexibility exercises to keep your muscles from getting too tight. Maybe you end your week with a set of interval sprints and a nice, long bike ride. If you change up your routine, working out becomes much more exciting.

Set Goals

While you can work out aimlessly, setting goals and attempting to meet them is a really fun way to motivate yourself. If you want to set goals, try getting a workout diary or journal where you can track how often you work out, the intensity of each activity, and how you felt. With this diary or journal, you can see how much you've improved over time.

While some people like to keep their workout diary secret, you can also get a simple whiteboard to track your progress. You can put it in your bedroom or on the wall where you can see it every day as a way to motivate yourself to keep going and continue your workout routine.

There are even phone applications for this that you can look up. If you're a runner or biker, see if you can find a GPS app that tracks your miles. If you like to do strength training, there are apps to track your strength workouts and help you stay on track for targeting each muscle group. There are plenty of free options available alongside paid ones, so choose the best tracker that works well for you.

Sneak Exercise Into Your Routine

Sometimes, it can be really hard to motivate yourself to work out. Keep in mind that this is normal, and there will be times when you just won't feel like doing that workout. On days when you are busy or have a lot of schoolwork to do, you can sneak exercise into your routine by parking at the back of the lot, walking to your friend's house instead of having your parents drive you, or walking on the treadmill while you read that chapter for history class.

Tips for a Safe Workout Plan

While it's important to push yourself and see how much you can improve your fitness, it's equally important to work out safely. For that reason, make sure you always drink water and eat enough calories to support your extra exercise. If you become too dehydrated or don't eat enough, you might get a headache and feel groggy.

If you're trying to set a new personal record for lifting or want to see if you can run that extra mile, make sure you have a workout buddy or someone who knows where you are and what you're doing. When running or biking, you could ask your friend to bike alongside you or have someone track your whereabouts on your phone. If you are unsure whether you can lift a certain amount of weight, you should have someone spotting you at the gym. Always be safe and know your limits!

Being an Athlete and Working Out: Do I Have To?

If you're an athlete who attends practice every day throughout the week, there's a good chance that you don't need to do any extra workout sessions besides what feels right. If you're in an especially cardio-heavy sport, it may be good to do some yoga on the weekends or go for a walk with your dog. These lower-impact activities allow you to rest your body and be prepared to hit it hard at practice the next week.

Unless your coach recommends extra workouts or ways to improve your game, you really don't need to work too hard if your off time. This is not to say that you shouldn't, but be aware that there are some dangers to working out way too much.

For example, if you take working out to the extreme, you could accidentally lose too much weight and fall behind in your expected growth. This may leave you feeling groggy, weak, and not great overall. If you want to thrive as a teenager, you need to make sure that you're balancing your workout routine with everything else in your life, and that includes food. In addition, too much exercise might interfere with your normal activities in school, and you may experience stress injuries or other health problems that could interfere with your ability to stay strong and be successful in your sport.

Most importantly, you want to make sure that you are eating enough calories to support any extra exercise. Your body needs a specific number of calories just to function on a normal basis. When you work out and burn more calories, you need to consume even more calories to maintain your body weight.

Now, you may be wondering how much you should be eating and *what* you should be eating, but that is something we'll save for the following sections, so read on!

CHAPTER 2:

HOW MUCH SLEEP IS TOO MUCH?

As you enter into your teenage years, we have already alluded to the fact that you will experience some changes. One of the changes that not many teenagers expect, or notice, is the difference in sleep patterns. For example, did you know that you will be more likely to stay up late and sleep in to the late hours of the morning? Well, this is part of transitioning into your teens, and we'll explain why this happens in the sections to follow.

The Teenage Sleep Shift: What to Expect

A common misconception about teenagers and sleep is that people seem to think that teenagers sleep in later because they're lazy. Actually, there is a change that happens in your brain that alters its chemistry and changes your dark and light exposure so much that it influences your circadian rhythm.

Now, you're probably thinking, "What the heck did they just say?" While it sounds complicated, the process is easy to explain. Essentially, circadian rhythm is a process in your brain that tells your body when it's time to sleep and when it's time to wake up. Generally, your circadian rhythm follows the 24-hour period of the sun. So, when the sun comes up, you are more likely to wake up, but when the sun goes down, you get sleepy and want to go to bed. Makes sense, right?

But when you're a teenager, your hormones tell you that you want to stay up later than you did before. You'll find yourself staying up later into the night and not really feeling like you want to go to bed. However, this also means that you need to sleep in later the next day to feel awake and energized. So, if you stay up late on a school night and still have to get up at 6:00 a.m. to get ready and catch the bus, you're going to feel a lot more tired.

Melatonin and Why it Matters

You may have heard of melatonin, but do you know that it's a naturally occurring hormone that plays an important role in helping you fall asleep? Melatonin is released naturally into the brain to tell your body when it's time to go to sleep. When the sun goes down, your brain will release melatonin as part of your circadian rhythm.

But why does this matter? When you hit your teenage years and your body starts to change, your hormones will tell melatonin to be released later and later in the night. This is a key reason why you don't feel as tired earlier as you once did. Melatonin will still be released, but it's released much later, which is why you might not want to go to sleep until 2 o'clock in the morning.

If school started at noon, this wouldn't be a problem. The real issue happens when you still need to get up early in the morning, but your body isn't letting you fall asleep until later into the night. This lack of sleep can make you feel tired and groggy during the day. But not to worry. There are some things you can do to help get better sleep.

How Much Sleep Do I Need?

As a teenager, you need between 8 and 10 hours of sleep every single night. If you get up every morning at 6:00, that means you need to be in bed by 8:00 p.m. for 10 hours of sleep or 10:00 p.m. for 8 hours of sleep. However, with wild schedules that include school, sports, homework, jobs, and more, getting enough sleep can be really hard. In fact, most teenagers only get between 6.5 to 7.5 hours of sleep each night. And there are plenty of teenagers who get even less sleep than that.

What Happens When You Don't Get Enough Sleep?

When you don't get enough sleep, you might experience chronic sleep deprivation. Chronic sleep deprivation essentially means that you never get enough sleep, and that starts to impact your body. You might start to feel tired, but not getting enough sleep can also increase your risk of anxiety, depression, and low self-esteem. Even more, not getting enough sleep can start to impact your grades, sports, and relationships. You might start to feel so tired that you miss your morning class, thus racking up a record of being late, which could get you into serious trouble at school.

There are many negative impacts of not getting enough sleep. Not only will you feel tired throughout the day, but you will also start to experience a host of other issues such as extreme cravings, headaches, and concentration problems. You may even start to get sick more often! So, what can you do to make sure you get enough sleep to feel your best and rock your teenage years?

Sleep Tips for the Busy Teenage Girl

One of the best tips for making sure you get enough sleep is to figure out why you aren't getting enough sleep. You already have more knowledge than most teenage girls because you now know how hormones impact your brain and make it so that you don't want to fall asleep. However, there are several other ways in which you can improve your sleep schedule and get more hours of rest.

Create a Bedtime Routine

One of the simplest ways to help get your body ready for sleep is to create a bedtime routine and stick to it. While this can be harder on weekends, this bedtime routine is probably one of your biggest tools in helping your body get more sleep.

Keep in mind that when you create a bedtime routine, it can take up to 4 weeks for your brain to make the necessary associations with your daily schedule. Now, that probably seems like a while, but it takes this long to create a habit, so make sure you stick with your routine and give yourself time to adjust. It may be a good idea to keep a sleep diary to track your sleep and see just how much you have improved over time!

The type of bedtime routine that you create depends on your own personal preferences and your schedule. Typically, you want to choose a time that is realistic for you to fall asleep. For instance, start with trying to go to bed at 10 o'clock each evening and work your way down from there if you feel like you need more sleep. If you need to set your bedtime routine earlier, you should plan on scaling it back 10 minutes earlier each week until you reach your ideal bedtime. You will find that your ideal bedtime is when you feel good as you wake up in the morning, so keep note of when that happens!

An important part of creating a bedtime routine is doing the same thing every single night. That is, after all, what a routine is, and it's important that you stick with it if you want to get to bed on time. In addition, it is every bit as important to wake up at the same time every day. Similar to setting a distinct bedtime, you should also set your alarm to the same time every morning. However, this can be difficult on weekends, so you can cut yourself some slack. But just know that waking up at the same time every day is the best way to maintain a good bedtime routine.

Now, for the fun part of creating that routine. You should choose a bedtime routine that is relaxing and enjoyable. For example, you can have a bath integrated into your bedtime routine. Soak in some lavender salts, get lost in your book, revisit your childhood, color, write in your journal, do some gentle yoga, meditate, or do whatever makes you feel good. It may take some time to find your ideal bedtime routine, so try out a few things to figure out what works best for you!

Avoid Screens

You may have noticed that we did not include watching television or using your phone as part of your bedtime routine. That, indeed, was intentional. This is because you should avoid looking at screens for **at least 1 hour** before you go to bed because screens can stimulate your brain and make it difficult to fall asleep.

In fact, the light that comes from your cell phone, TV, computer, or any other type of screen can stimulate your brain's sleep-wake cycle (remember the circadian rhythm!) and make it so that your brain thinks it's time to stay awake. Instead, either keep your room dark or use low light as you are getting ready to sleep.

Stay Away From Caffeine

While you may or may not have already started to drink coffee, it is important to stay away from caffeine and any other stimulant, such as caffeinated tea, soft drinks, and energy drinks before you go to bed. Because caffeine is used to help your body stay alert and awake, drinking caffeine in the afternoon or evening can definitely impact your ability to fall asleep. So, stick to herbal tea, water, or hot cocoa before you go to bed.

Be Active During the Day

We bet you didn't think activity and exercise would have come back so quickly, huh? Well, having a regular workout routine and staying active during the day is a great way to make sure that your body is tired enough to fall asleep at night.

Even so, you should not work out late into the evening or before you go to bed. Since working out can help you feel energized, exercising right before bed may not be the best idea. Instead, work out in the morning or the afternoon to give your body time to cool down afterwards.

Design the "Dreamiest" Bedroom

Along with designing your dream bedtime routine, you should also prepare your bedroom to be the most calming and relaxing place possible. If you have too much stimulation or bright lights in your bedroom, it can be difficult to fall asleep. Instead, try to decorate your room as if you were creating your dream meditation area or tranquil living space.

You can stock your room with fluffy pillows, comfortable blankets, low lights, soft-noise machines, and relaxing colors to help get your body in the mindset for sleep. Setting up this comfortable sleep environment is a fun way to guarantee that you have a place where you can fall blissfully asleep. All in all, you need your beauty sleep, so keep your bedroom perfectly decorated to help you fall into peaceful dreams.

CHAPTER 3:

MASTERING HEALTH AND HYGIENE

Nobody wants to be smelly. Let's face it—we've all had that moment when you wonder if that smell is coming from you or you've sat next to a person who clearly forgot to put on deodorant. Luckily, there are some easy ways to smell good and master your own health and hygiene.

What is Hygiene?

Having good hygiene means that you keep your body clean and maintain healthy habits to stay safe from germs and other microbes that can cause disease. Learning how to be hygienic is an important life skill and one that you will hopefully engage for the rest of your life. If you don't take care of your body, you might not like the consequences later in life.

Hygiene habits are super important for several reasons. While smelling good should be a priority for many reasons, two major benefits are staying free of germs and avoiding awkward (and smelly) social interactions. Firstly, it is important to keep clean so that you can keep your body free of harmful germs that can make you sick. We're not just talking about the germs that can be on your hands, breathed in through your nose, or accidentally enter through your eyes; we're also talking about the bad germs that can lead to tooth decay, skin infections, and even fungus.

Without proper hygiene, you might also find that your smelly body odor puts off potential friends and makes it challenging to find someone to sit next to during lunch. No one wants to sit next to a person who smells really bad, so make sure you shower, wash your hands, brush your teeth, and otherwise maintain good hygiene.

How to Build a Hygiene Routine

While every person's hygiene routine will be a little bit different depending on their activity levels and body, there are a couple of habits that all teenage girls should do if they want to be stink free and healthy.

Showering and Bathing

Although it may be inconvenient and take precious time that you'd rather spend with friends, you should shower or bathe every day. Now, this does not need to be an intense scrub-a-dub-dub shower, but you should clean the sweat and dirt off your body each day. You don't even need to wash your hair every single day unless you like it or your parents prefer it. Depending on how much oil you have in your hair and the texture, you may choose to be on a different hair-washing schedule.

Hair Care

The key to having clean and oil-free hair is to wash it regularly or use hair products that are the best for your hair type. For example, some people have dandruff and need specific hair products to keep the dandruff at bay, while others need shampoo that prevents oily hair. Further, you should find hair products that are good for your type of hair. Whether you have thick and coarse hair, curly hair, or straight hair, there is a good hair product out there for you.

If you are having a hard time finding shampoos and conditioners that are the best for your hair type, try talking to your salon stylist or see if your parent, caregiver, friends, or siblings have any suggestions. However, you should keep in mind that it might take a couple of tries to find a product that works for you.

Another important part of hair care is brushing. You should brush or comb your hair according to what's best for your hair. Similar to finding the right shampoo and conditioner, you might need to play around with brushes and combs to find the right tools. For ladies with thicker curly hair, a comb might work best, but for the teenager with straight and thinner hair, you might find that a bristled brush works the best. You should use a comb or brush that feels good on your hair and doesn't pull your hair out.

If you do get tangles, you can use detangler spray and a few other tricks to keep the knots away. Whether you find that braiding your hair at night helps make hair maintenance easier or you prefer to wrap your hair, there are many ways to protect it. Another simple way to prevent knots, especially for girls with curly hair, is to sleep with a silk pillowcase. Oddly enough, the silk in the pillowcase helps to keep tangles to a minimum.

Finally, make sure you get haircuts or treatments to maintain your hair or cut off any split ends that limit your hair growth. Not only should you go into the salon to take care of your hair professionally, but the stylists are hair experts who can help you pick out the perfect hair-care products.

Dental Care

Your teeth need to be taken care of meticulously if you want to still have them when you're older. You've probably heard this threat before, but trust us, it is real. If you don't brush your teeth and go to the dentist regularly, you might need to get replacements later in life.

You should brush your teeth at least twice each day. In the morning, brushing your teeth can get rid of morning breath, and the minty taste can be a refreshing wake-up call. At the end of the day, brushing your teeth can get rid of any food that is left over from eating, and it prepares your teeth for a good night's rest. In addition to brushing, you need to floss your teeth at least once a day. We have all been to the dentist and likely lied about how much we floss our teeth, thinking we get away with it. However, when your gums bleed at the dentist, they know that you were lying and clearly not flossing. So, avoid this embarrassment and floss away.

Personal Hygiene Products

You don't need to spend hundreds of dollars on personal hygiene products, but there are a few items that every teenage girl should have in her bathroom and bedroom. These necessities include shampoo, soap and body wash, conditioner, facial products, lotions, and deodorant.

As we mentioned above, shampoo is important for hair care. In fact, it can be one of the best defenses against oily or greasy hair. During puberty, you might find that your hair feels greasier than it did before, which means you might have to shower or bathe more often than you're used to. Find a good shampoo to keep your hair happy and healthy.

Soap and body wash are important for keeping your body clean and scrubbing off any excess dirt or sweat. This is the best way to fight body odor, especially if you are an active teenager who participates in sports and other physical activities. You don't need anything fancy; basic soap should do the trick. However, some of the fancier body washes have moisturizing components that can be good for your skin.

Conditioner is important for hydrating your hair and making it shiny and soft. If you have a problem with tangles, conditioner can be your best friend. You should let the conditioner sit in your hair for a few minutes after rubbing it in so that it has enough time to sink into your hair follicles.

If you want soft and smooth skin, lotion will be your best friend. You can find a healthy body lotion that leaves your skin feeling great at pretty much any of your local drug stores. Last but certainly not least is deodorant. This tube will likely be one of the products that absolutely saves your life and prevents all stink that comes along with your teenage years. Not only can you get deodorant that keeps you smelling fresh and clean, but many deodorants are also antiperspirants that keep your armpits from sweating.

Acne Tips

Whiteheads, blackheads, papules, nodules, and cysts, oh my! Did you know that each of these are a type of acne? Did you even know that there was more than one kind? Well, acne comes in many fun-filled shapes and sizes that need to be carefully managed. Unfortunately, some girls will get more acne than others, and some may not get acne at all. Truly, this isn't fair. But what you can do is take care of your face and body to help keep the acne to a minimum.

The best thing you can do for your acne is to wash your face with oil-free facial cleanser. You should also avoid touching your face or pressing your phone against it. Bottom line is that the more you touch your face, the more you are welcoming acne. In addition, being extra stressed and anxious can actually make your acne worse. In later sections, we'll talk about how to properly manage your stress, so keep on reading to learn how good coping skills can make your body feel better.

If you've tried every good facial cleanser in the world and still have difficulty with acne, you may want to try something a little stronger. There are some nonprescription topical ointments that you can get for your skin. These ointments and lotions usually have some sort of acetic acid or benzyl peroxide that is effective in treating moderate acne. But keep in mind that these products can take a few weeks to start working.

If you've tried these over-the-counter treatments and still struggle with acne, you can contact your doctor or dermatologist for a prescription medication. While some girls will do perfectly fine with a stronger ointment from the store, others may need to get a medical prescription.

Other Important Hygiene Tips

There are many hygiene tips that likely seem intuitive, and this is a good thing. Hopefully, you have been doing most of these already and will continue to do them as you navigate your teens. A couple of other important tips that can help you be a master at hygiene include taking care of your fingernails and toenails. Of course, you can file and paint your toenails and fingernails all the time, but it's also important to simply groom by clipping them when they get too long and taking care of any hangnails. That way, you can avoid biting your nails and causing the skin around them to become inflamed.

Another obvious tip is that you should change your underwear and socks every day. Yup, you should not simply turn a pair inside out and call it good. Instead, get a fresh pair of underwear and clean socks to wear. Although you do not need to wash all your clothes after every single use, especially if you only wore them for a little bit, it's best to regularly wash your clothes and do laundry.

The Art of Healthy Eating

Eating healthy is every bit as important as keeping your body clean and exercising. Not only does healthy eating allow you to maintain a good body weight, but eating the right foods can help you feel good and give you energy. Some of the best healthy-eating tips for teenage girls include:

- Eat three meals a day and have healthy snacks in between.
- Eat plenty of fiber.
- Try to avoid too much sugar and salt.
- Drink lots of water.
- Eat balanced meals of grains, protein, fruits, and vegetables.
- Eat when you are hungry, and stop eating when you're full.

When creating a balanced meal, you should have all of the food groups represented so that your meals have full nutritional value. That means you need to eat a good mix of grains, protein, fruits, veggies, and dairy products. To get a better idea of what's included in each of these food groups, check out the picture below.

The Truth About Fad Diets

As you approach your teens, you might start to hear more about quick and easy weight-loss fads. In fact, your friends might be doing them already and making you feel like you have to do the same. While we won't deny that fad diets can help you drop weight, that weight will not stay off for long. Not only will you likely gain all the weight back with these quick fixes, but they are incredibly unhealthy for your body and can even be dangerous.

You can spot a fad diet quickly because they always promote how easy they are and how fast you will lose weight. Keep in mind that the weight that you lose is typically water weight. You cannot physically lose more than 2 to 3 pounds each week no matter what you do, so these fad diets are nothing but a scam.

Healthy Things You Should Do

We have now touched on several things that you should do to maintain a healthy lifestyle. Not only should you get regular exercise, but making sure you get enough sleep and eating a healthy diet are also incredibly important health practices. As we continue going over more ways that you can survive your teenage years, we will begin to touch on the changes that your body will start to go through as a teenager. This will include a discussion on how to cope with stress, anxiety, and other mental-health challenges.

CHAPTER 4:

LET'S TALK ABOUT PUBERTY

Puberty is the star of the show when it comes to your teenage years. During puberty, you will experience many changes in your body and your mind. While these changes seem intimidating, just know that every teenage girl has to go through them, and you are not alone.

What is Puberty?

At its core, puberty is the process that every human being goes through as their body prepares to become physically mature. These natural changes to your body are all because of natural substances that are commonly known as hormones.

Typically, girls will begin puberty between the ages of 8 and 13. However, puberty is a long process that lasts for several years. Your body may not be done changing until the end of your teens. Everyone is different, so some girls may begin puberty earlier than others, and some girls may continue puberty much later than their peers.

Puberty itself is full of physical and emotional changes that can seem scary. However, these changes are normal, and your body knows what to do. The best thing you can do right now is understand the changes that are coming. That way, you will be prepared to face your period like the woman you are about to become!

Bodily Changes

There are many changes to your body that will happen during puberty. First, your hands and feet will start to grow. In fact, you might feel a little clumsy because the rest of your body might take its time to catch up. Typically, girls will reach their full height about 2 years after they start puberty. Once you start noticing these changes, it'll all be over in just a few short years.

Your body isn't just growing up; it's growing and developing in other places too. As girls hit puberty, their bodies begin to become curvier in the hips and breast areas. For many girls, growing breasts can be awkward and even stressful. It's a time of major change, and not everyone is comfortable with breasts.

Breasts will change in size and color and may grow hair. This is all normal. The size and shape of breasts often runs in your family, so your genetics may give you clues as to what your developing body will eventually look like. For some girls, this information is comforting and makes the entire process easier to endure.

As your breasts start to develop, you will find that you need to wear a bra. While many girls will start with training bras, you will quickly upgrade to the typical sports bra or generic bra. You can easily measure yourself with a tape measure, or you can try on bra sizes until you find the right fit. Your bra should feel comfortable and not be too tight or too loose.

However, the changing body is not done at height, breast, and hip development. In fact, you will start to notice a lot of body hair. While it may seem odd, body hair will develop in places that you may not expect it. You will start to notice more or thicker hair in your armpits, on your legs, and in the pubic area near your genitals. Many girls choose to shave their armpits and legs, but this is completely up to you and your own preferences.

Mood and Emotional Changes

Not only does your body change during puberty, but your emotions will change too. Although everyone is different, every teenage girl likely goes through some sort of mood or emotional change. Furthermore, these emotional changes vary wildly from person to person.

Some teens find that they begin to have a better sense of their identity and may become more interested in boys. Others may become more conscious of their changing bodies and begin to feel insecure. Some teenage girls want to take on more responsibilities and become more independent, but others find that they prefer to stay home and enjoy their alone time. Your preferences are your own, so take this time to figure out who you are and what you like to do!

Why are these mood and emotional changes happening? Well, it's all in the brain. During puberty, some of the neural connections in your brain continue to get stronger while others get weaker. This means that some of your new skills will seem easier, and you may no longer find former activities interesting. For example, you may decide that you want to become a soccer star and leave softball behind. As you practice your soccer skills and get better, you might not be as good at softball as you once were simply because you stopped practicing.

These changes in the brain will happen all throughout your life, but you're most likely to notice significant changes during puberty. You might even experience some mood swings where you feel angry, sad, happy, energized, lazy, and more all within the same day (or even the same hour). These mood swings can last several hours or days. Again, everyone will be different, and you might not even notice the mood changes unless they are pointed out to you by your close friends and family.

Menstruation: AKA Your Period

Among the most overwhelming changes is the beginning of menstruation, commonly known as your period. Every month, the lining of your uterus will thicken with blood and an egg will be released from one of your ovaries. If that egg is not fertilized by sperm, the lining within your uterus will shed. This shedding is the blood that you will see coming through your vagina during menstruation.

Periods can be scary because it seems like there is a lot of blood coming out of a place where it shouldn't be. However, it's actually only a few tablespoons. Typically, your period will be heavier the first day or so and will get lighter as the week goes on. While some girls may have shorter periods, others may have their periods for up to 7 days.

As you go through puberty and start menstruation, you may notice that you have a very irregular period. Irregular periods are normal in the first 3 years, and it will get better and more predictable over time.

CHAPTER 5:

REPRODUCTIVE HEALTH AND WELLNESS

Now that you're reaching the age when you'll start getting your period, it's important to know how to take care of your reproductive system and your body as it progresses through puberty. This involves understanding the symptoms of your period and learning the best ways to take care of yourself while you are menstruating.

What to Expect From Your Period

There are several period symptoms that many girls experience. However, each teenager will be different, and you may even experience some symptoms at different times than others. In fact, it's not uncommon to have varying symptoms with each one of your periods. Even so, you will likely notice some symptoms are present more often than others.

Premenstrual syndrome, commonly known as PMS, is the catchall term for the emotional and physical symptoms that happen either before or during your period. Many of these symptoms include moodiness, anxiety, bloating, acne, sadness, and more. PMS is what likely makes you want to bite your best friend's head off even though she only did something mildly irritating, and PMS might explain why you start crying because you ran out of pickles in the fridge. Even though PMS can be annoying, there are plenty of ways to manage it.

Cramps

One of the banes to a woman's experience is cramps. Many girls have cramps along with their periods, especially during the first 2 days. While some girls will have such light cramps that they barely notice them, others may need to take a sick day and lie on the couch just to deal with the pain. Whether you are the former or the latter, there are many tricks that you can do to help with the annoying pain of cramps.

If you have bad cramps, you can start by taking some pain relievers such as ibuprofen. This simple over-the-counter medication can alleviate the pain and make you feel more comfortable. Another trick that many girls enjoy is to take a warm heating pad and put it on top of your pelvic region right below your stomach. The warmth can reduce the severity of your cramps, and the heat will likely feel good regardless.

Backaches

Along with cramps on the front side of your body, some girls also get backaches. These backaches usually occur low and feel more like a pressure than a pain. Even so, they can be incredibly uncomfortable. Similar to dealing with cramps, you can take some ibuprofen or put a heating pad on your back to help with the pain and discomfort.

Acne

As we talked about in the sections above, acne can occur during puberty. There are many types of acne, but regardless of how severe your acne is, it is annoying. You can help combat acne by washing your face and stopping yourself from touching your face, but sometimes the hormones win and you get it anyway.

Many girls will get acne during their monthly cycle, and there isn't much you can do to stop it besides letting the acne run its course. Even so, wash your face, and avoid popping the zits if you can.

Breast Tenderness

Another common symptom of menstruation is breast tenderness. Most commonly, breast tenderness feels like an uncomfortable pressure that can be alleviated with some ibuprofen. When your breasts are developing, it's likely that they'll feel tender a lot of the time.

The Flow

Menstruation, commonly known as your period, is the main event of your monthly cycle. When your period happens, blood will exit your uterus as the uterine lining sheds through your vagina. Once you start your period, you have about a week before it's over. The heaviness of a period differs depending on the person, so the supplies you use to manage your period may be determined by your flow.

How Long Do Periods Last?

The average length of a period is about 5 days. However, some girls may have shorter and lighter periods, while others may have heavier and longer periods. The length and heaviness of your period may be different than the people you know, but there is a wide range of normal, and it's not something you need to worry about. In fact, you may notice different period symptoms and levels of flow depending on the month!

Most girls will get their period once every 4 to 5 weeks. Anything within this range is normal, but remember that it may take a few years for your period schedule to become regular. If you've been getting your period irregularly for a few years and you still don't get it every month, it may be best to go see your doctor and see what's going on with your body.

You will likely have a period every month until you reach menopause. Menopause is when women reach an age at which they are no longer able to have children. This usually occurs between the ages of 45 and 55. When you hit menopause, your periods will permanently stop.

In addition, women will not get their periods when they are pregnant. Because your body focuses on the development of another human being, it will not release any more eggs, and you will not have a period for the entire time that you are pregnant.

How to Manage Your Period

Once you've gotten used to menstruation, you will find the ways to best manage your period and PMS symptoms. However, there are several options available to help with the blood flow during your period. Although the most commonly used materials are tampons and pads, the menstrual cup has quickly become popular among many teenage girls.

Tampons, Menstrual Cups, or Pads?

You can find tampons, pads, and even menstrual cups in the female-hygiene aisle of your local grocery and drug stores.

Pads are absorbent strips that temporarily attach to your underwear. Pads are typically made of cotton, and they come in various shapes, sizes, and thicknesses. Many girls will start by using pads and graduate to other forms of feminine-hygiene products. In addition, some girls may use tampons during the day and switch to pads at night.

Tampons are often considered more convenient than pads because the tampon is inserted into the vagina to absorb blood. Instead of hoping that the blood will be soaked up by the pad, a tampon absorbs blood before it leaves the vagina. However, you don't want to leave a tampon in for more than 8 hours because it can lead to a serious infection known as toxic shock syndrome.

A feminine-hygiene product that has quickly gained traction is the menstrual cup. This cup is inserted into the vagina and holds blood until you remove and empty it. These cups are generally made of silicone and are reusable.

What to Wear During Your Period

For most of your period, there is no need to change your style of dress or what you wear. However, some girls do find that loose-fitting clothing such as sweatpants and sweatshirts more comfortable during their period. Looser-fitting clothing is often a lot more comfortable, especially if you have bloating and cramping.

If you're worried about getting blood on your clothes, you should avoid wearing pants that are light in color. While it's always a bummer to get blood on your pants, the blood is a lot less visible and can even be unnoticeable if you wear darker pants.

When you go to bed, just make sure you are wearing clothes that help keep your pad or other feminine-hygiene product in place so that you don't have an accident. In addition, some girls find that placing a towel underneath them while they sleep can help reduce the likelihood of leakage. If you have a heavy period, these tricks can help save your sheets.

Period Self-Care

While understanding your period symptoms and knowing what you should wear while on your period is important, the most important part of being on your period is taking care of yourself. Because many girls experience uncomfortable symptoms and side effects, making sure you are relaxed and comfortable is critical.

While you are on your period, you can take a hot bath to help with the cramps, go for a walk to move your body, watch some of your favorite television shows during an easy night, or curl up with a book and a hot cup of tea. Most importantly, you should focus on doing the activities that make you feel happy and allow you to avoid stress.

Staying hydrated is also important during your period. Not only does drinking water help avoid hormonal breakouts, but drinking enough water can help with your circulation, digestion, and removing the toxins in your body. Your body also tends to get hunger and thirst confused, so drinking water can aid in curbing those cravings.

While we're not saying that unhealthy food is the answer to everything, sometimes it feels good to eat some chocolate or indulge in your favorite foods to treat yourself while you're menstruating. We absolutely give you the okay to do this!

CHAPTER 6:

HOW TO MANAGE FIGHTS WITH FRIENDS

Drama, drama, drama. Do we even need to say more? By now, you've probably already experienced some drama and even fights with your best friend. However, this may not get any better going into your teens. In fact, as you and your friends start to figure out your own identities and who you want to be, you might find yourself getting into more arguments and fights than ever before.

One fight shouldn't ruin a friendship. In fact, getting into disagreements and arguments is part of building a stronger relationship with your friends. You're not going to agree with everything someone else does, so this is part of discovering your values and who you really are. There are definitely good and bad ways to manage fights with friends. To learn how to navigate drama and come out of a fight as friends, keep on reading!

Why Are Friends Mean?

Girls can be mean. Heck, the movie *Mean Girls* wasn't some random movie idea that was pulled out of a hat. During your teenage years and in high school, you'll deal with some mean girls and drama that you thought only existed in the movies. However, there are usually a few different reasons why girls are mean. Typically, miscommunication, the other girl's low self-esteem, and jealousy have something to do with the meanness.

Miscommunication as the Culprit

Miscommunication can be anything from your friend misinterpreting something you said to your sarcasm not getting picked up over text. Even further, sometimes other girls can repeat what you said about someone in a way that doesn't actually represent what you meant in the first place. When this happens, miscommunication is likely to be the underlying reason of your fight. This can often be resolved with a clear conversation.

She Has Low Self-Esteem

Typically, bullies and mean girls are cruel because they have lower self-esteem. While it does seem weird that some girls will pick on other girls simply because they're jealous, this is commonly the case. Sometimes, your friend or the girl you're fighting with might feel inferior to you, which is why they stirred up drama about you in the first place. There is usually some reason why this person started the drama, but it could be anything. It could be a fight over a boy, jealousy over your clothes, feeling inferior to you in sports, or any other reason.

What to Do When You and Your Friends Fight

Having a fight with your friends is inevitable. Yet there are some things you can do to resolve conflicts and make sure that you come out of the fight with your friendship intact. As you go through each section and learn how to deal with fights with friends, understand that every single situation is going to be different and that one technique may not be enough to solve a specific fight. Instead, knowing different ways to resolve conflict will empower you to use them when you feel they're the right move.

Give Her Space

Sometimes, you just need to give your friends some space. Time is one of the best ways to make drama fizzle out. In the moment, arguments can get hot, words can cut deep, and fights can get ugly. So, instead of trying to solve every conflict immediately, give your friend some time to cool off and process the fight. Quite honestly, you probably need some time and space to get over the fight too. That way, you can come back together and resolve the conflict calmly.

Set a Time to Talk it Out

Because it's a good idea to give your friend some time and space to process a fight or something that happened between you, setting a time to sit down and talk can be a powerful move. You should do this in a quiet space where you can be alone and talk to each other uninterrupted. While this can be done over text, we wouldn't advise it. Sometimes, information and tone can get lost over text message, which can make situations worse. Instead, find a place such as a coffee shop or simply go for a walk to talk it out. If you can talk in person, you can avoid any further miscommunication.

Make Sure You Both Speak to Your Experience

When you have a fight, it can be all too easy to assume how the other person is feeling and what the other person did.

When you set a time to talk to the friend you're fighting with, make sure that both of you get a chance to speak about your own experiences. During a fight, words can be exaggerated, lies can be told, and false assumptions can be made. Instead of inventing some false narrative about your friend, make sure you listen to what her experience was so that you can fully understand what happened.

In addition, you should also get a chance to speak about how you interpreted the situation. In a fight, your feelings and experiences matter, and you should come to a place where both of you feel good about the situation. This can involve some compromising, apologizing, and explaining, especially if one of you misinterpreted the situation.

The Power of "I Feel" Statements

Too often, the conversation that you have with your friend and any attempt to make up after a fight can turn into an all-out blame session. When this happens, your friend, or you, depending on which side of the argument you're on, can feel like they are being attacked. When your friend is feeling attacked, the conversation will never go well because they are more likely to be defensive or shut down completely.

Instead of blaming someone, use "I feel" statements to describe how the argument or fight made you feel. This will direct the conversation toward your own emotions and avoid blaming the other person. It doesn't matter if the fight was their fault in the first place; this is the best way to manage conflict and make up after a fight.

When you use "I feel" statements, focus on your friend's behavior and explain how what they did made you feel. Mention how their behavior impacts you and other people, and offer up ways they can do better next time.

Don't Spread Gossip

When you're in a fight, the worst thing you can do is go off and tell all your friends what happened. If you spread gossip about the fight or start telling lies about your friend, it can quickly get out of hand and the fight could get even worse. Because gossip can spread so quickly, it can damage the relationship with your friend to the point that you may not be able to resolve the fight.

Instead, you should focus on keeping the fight between yourselves and resolving the conflict before you go to anyone else. Of course, you should never have to deal with the fight on your own, and you can go to a trusted friend, sibling, or parent if you need any advice on how to solve the argument. You can absolutely talk to someone about what happened so that you can figure out the best way to make it right; just make sure you leave the gossip out of it and maybe avoid telling that one friend who cannot seem to keep a secret.

Know When to Walk Away

Unfortunately, some fights can bring out drama and sides of people in a way that makes it difficult to go back to being their friend. Whether this is a single argument that you cannot get past, or if you find yourself constantly fighting or having problems with one friend, you might have to walk away from that friendship. If you find yourself in a toxic relationship where you constantly feel unappreciated or unvalued, it may be time to fade that friend out of your life.

While this is never an easy decision and can be difficult to do, there are some ways to deal with toxic friends and unhealthy friend relationships. That information is reserved for the next chapter!

CHAPTER 7:

DEALING WITH PEER PRESSURE AND FRENEMIES

Basically, a peer is your friend or anyone who is your same age and could potentially be your friend. But if some of these people are your friends, why do they sometimes ask you to do things that you don't feel comfortable with? Why do your friends or the people around you sometimes make you feel like you need to do something just to fit in? Simple: That's peer pressure.

What is Peer Pressure?

Peer pressure is essentially when a friend or someone you know makes you feel like you need to do something in order to be accepted or fit in with that particular group. This person or group of people might make you feel like you need to do certain things, say certain things, or treat people a certain way just so that you can hang out with them.

Depending on what you are being convinced to do, peer pressure can feel downright icky. In fact, negative peer pressure can often make you feel guilty or disappointed with yourself for doing something that goes against what you believe in. This is why peer pressure is something that you should try to avoid. You will probably always have to deal with some amount of peer pressure, so you must learn not only how to spot it but also how to deal with it.

Even though peer pressure comes in many forms, some common examples of peer pressure include:

- Dressing a certain way
- Copying someone else's work
- Letting other people copy your work
- Feeling like you need to exclude someone out of social events
- Driving dangerously
- Using drugs or alcohol
- Stealing or shoplifting
- Bullying or cyberbullying
- Vandalizing
- Eating certain foods or dieting
- Posting misleading or false images on your social media
- Going to parties or social events you don't want to attend

What's important to know about peer pressure is that sometimes it's not intentional. While there are instances when friends — or people who you believe are your friends — make you feel like you have to do something just to fit in, sometimes it's the case that you simply think you need to do something just to fit in with your friend group. For example, one of the most common activities associated with peer pressure is drinking alcohol. Although you may think that everyone is drinking alcohol, only about 29 percent of teens ages 12 to 20 actually report drinking.

So, sometimes we just think we need to do something to fit in when it's perfectly acceptable not to. Even so, it's important to find ways to deal with peer pressure so that you don't get roped into doing something you don't actually want to do. That said, let's learn some more about peer pressure!

Peer Pressure Isn't Always Bad

Peer pressure can be positive or negative. When we think of peer pressure, we commonly think of the bad type of peer pressure, or the negative peer pressure that makes you do something that you don't really want to do. However, peer pressure can also be positive because it can push you to do your best and reach goals that you never thought you could attain.

Some examples of positive peer pressure could be going to practice for sports so that you get better at your athletics, or it could be getting dragged into a study group with your friends so that you're more prepared for the social studies test coming up. Generally, you know peer pressure is positive when something good comes out of it. However, positive peer pressure's evil cousin, the negative type of peer pressure, is something that you need to learn how to deal with.

How to Deal with Peer Pressure

Unfortunately, you will likely come across peer pressure or hang out with people who make you feel like you need to do things just to be accepted. When that happens, there are several different techniques you can use in order to resist. By learning these techniques, you can be your confident, fabulous self and only do things that you actually want to do.

Know Your Boundaries

The first step to dealing with peer pressure is understanding your values and your boundaries. While you probably already have an idea about what you would do and what you wouldn't, it's worth it to reflect on your own boundaries and figure out what you would be comfortable with. Once you figure out your boundaries, you're ready to deal with peer pressure. If a friend or friend group consistently asks you to step outside of your boundaries in a way that you don't like, you can absolutely say no.

Be Confident

Confidence is key in nearly every situation. When you have to tell your friends that you're not comfortable with something, do so in a confident way. Although you will likely get pushback from friends because that is what peer pressure is, being confident in your own answers and your own decisions is an incredibly important skill to have in general. Plus, it can be very useful in these situations.

Open Communication

Having friends that you feel comfortable talking to about anything is important, especially in situations involving peer pressure. When it comes to having close friends, the ones that you want to keep around are the ones who make you feel comfortable and happy with who you are. If you do have a friend you don't feel comfortable having an open and honest conversation with, it might not be a very good friendship (or a healthy one at that).

If you're feeling pressured, you should feel comfortable enough to tell your friends that you don't want to do what they're asking you to do. When you are open about how you feel, your friends can understand where your boundaries lie.

Learn to Say No

One of the most important skills that you will ever learn in your life is how to say no. You should never have to apologize when you say no because you are your own person with the freedom to do whatever the heck you want. So, learn how to say no so that you can stand your ground and not give in to peer pressure.

Always Have a Way Out

Not every instance of peer pressure can be avoided or communicated ahead of time. Sometimes, peer pressure can show up out of nowhere, and you can find yourself all of a sudden in a very uncomfortable situation. So, make sure you always have some sort of emergency action plan or a person you can call for help. It doesn't matter if you have to text your sibling, call your parents, or email your grandma — make sure you always have an escape plan!

Develop a Secret Code with Your Parents

While it might not be the coolest option, there is absolutely nothing wrong with getting your parents or guardians involved in a peer-pressure situation. If you have a friend or friend group who is starting to make you do things that you really aren't comfortable with, you can absolutely tell a trusted adult about the situation.

In fact, having a secret code that you can either call, text, or tell your parents can be a very useful tool when it comes to peer pressure. If you're out with your friends and something happens, you can simply text your parents the secret code, and they can find a way to come pick you up. Your secret code could be anything from "banana" to "furry burrito," so get creative!

Be Yourself

Although open and honest communication, having an emergency plan, and learning how to say no are all incredibly valuable in the face of peer pressure, one of the most important tools that you have in avoiding peer pressure is being yourself. There is always a balance between peer pressure and peer influence, but you should never give into something just because your friends want you to. Instead of having to worry about peer pressure, focus on being yourself and surrounding yourself with people who love you for you.

What is a Frenemy?

Not all friendships are good friendships. Although that might sound strange, it also might make total sense. In fact, we would almost guarantee that we all have (or at least have had) that friend who makes us feel kind of icky or takes advantage. You might even be really close with this person, but the friendship clearly isn't the healthiest. In addition, being around this person might even make you feel bad about yourself.

Another common term for a frenemy is a toxic friendship. Instead of making you feel like you belong and are accepted, toxic friends can make you feel bad about yourself or like you need to do things in order to earn their friendship. Sometimes, these frenemies can put you down, manipulate you, purposefully leave you out, or do other things to make you feel bad. This can happen in person to your face, but it also commonly happens on social media.

Because we will encounter or have encountered this type of friend, it's important to learn how to judge the health of your friendships and know when one isn't doing you any favors. This can be difficult, but you need to know when to let a friendship fizzle out.

How to Determine the "Health" of Your Friendship

It might sound a little bit strange, but you need to determine the "health" of your friendship to figure out if you're in a toxic friendship or dealing with a good one. Basically, the health of your friendship describes how spending time with that individual makes you feel and whether or not you seem empowered and confident around that person. Friends should always bring you up and make you feel good about yourself, not tear you down and make you feel like you aren't enough. If you're experiencing the latter with a certain friend, then that relationship might be toxic.

The first step to figuring out the health of your friendship is to ask yourself questions about how a certain friend makes you feel. If you're trying to figure out whether a friend is toxic or not, check out the graphic below. You should also ask yourself:

- Do I look forward to spending time with this person?
- How does this person make me feel about myself when I am with them or talking to them?
- After a conversation, how do I feel about myself?

- Does this friendship make me feel empowered?
- Do I feel drained after hanging out or having a conversation with this person?

Once you learn how to spot a toxic friend, you might find yourself examining all your friendships. You should know that there will always be some ups and downs within friendships, but the strong ones will always end up being positive and make you feel good at the end of the day. Remember that friends can fight, but the good friends are ones you look forward to hanging out with and who make you feel good about being yourself.

How to Find a New Friend Group

Toxic friends don't need to stay in your life. In fact, you will likely be much happier once that person is no longer hurting you on a regular basis. Instead, surround yourself with people who make you feel good about who you are.

However, this may also mean that you need to find a way to meet other people and establish a new group of friends. Finding new friends can seem hard, but there are many ways to meet new people and find new besties.

Make a List of Friends Outside the Toxic Group

Most likely, the toxic friend that you are trying to spend less time with is not your only friend. So, start by making a list of friends that you have outside of the toxic friend or group. You might be surprised. This list may be much longer than you thought it would be! Maybe you have a friend on the volleyball team who you practice with after school, or maybe there's another girl you sit next to on the bus.

Just start making a list of all the people that you hang out with or find yourself constantly running into. After you've made your list, highlight the people you're comfortable talking to, and maybe you can even ask them to hang out after school or on the weekends. Or just start by actually getting their number or following them on social media!

Find Ways to Spend Time with Other Friends

Sometimes, you have hung out with your rather toxic friend because they are the most convenient one to be around. Everyone has really busy schedules, especially if you're going to school, in sports, in clubs, or working. That said, it might take some planning to find times to hang out with other friends.

Yet finding ways to hang out with people could be as simple as sitting with someone new at lunch, making study dates with new people, or coming to school a little bit earlier.

Join New Clubs, Teams, or Extracurricular Activities

When all else fails, the best way to meet new people is to try new things. It doesn't matter if you decide to go out for the debate team, join the cross-country team, or run for student council. Trying something new and surrounding yourself with new faces can be one of the best ways to form connections and friendships.

CHAPTER 8:

MANAGING STRESS AND CONQUERING COPING SKILLS

Your teenage years can take you on one of the wildest emotional-rollercoaster rides of your entire life. Not only are you encountering a wide range of emotions, but the amount of social pressure, schoolwork, and increasing number of responsibilities can make everything hard to manage at times. For that reason, you need to become a master at coping skills. Coping skills can be used for nearly anything or any reason, but it's up to you to figure out what helps you relax and unwind.

Stress can come from literally anywhere. In fact, there are even good types of stress (eustress) and negative types of stress (distress). Whereas eustress refers to any stressor that ultimately energizes you or motivates you, negative stress can make you feel drained, irritated, and downright icky. There are several types of distress that you will come across as a teenager if you haven't experienced them already. Some of the most common causes of stress in your teenage years include:

- Changes in your body, such as puberty
- Fights with friends or problems with people at school
- Moving or changing schools

- Taking on too many activities, sports, or clubs
- Feeling as though you are subjected to excessively high expectations
- Death of a family member or loved one
- Negative thoughts or feelings about yourself
- Demands from school or frustration with academics
- Separation or divorce of your parents
- Living in an unsafe neighborhood
- Experiencing family financial problems

All of these can be sources of stress in your life, and unfortunately, you can't always predict when they're going to happen. That said, you should always have some coping skills in your back pocket to pull out if you experience any significant stressors.

Mental Illness vs. Mental Wellness

Many people get mental illness and mental wellness confused. Although they may sound the same, they are quite different. Whereas mental illness is used to describe various medical diagnoses, mental wellness describes your psychological, social, and emotional well-being. Simply said, mental wellness is your ability to be happy in your daily life, manage your emotions, and cultivate meaningful relationships.

When it comes to coping skills, the focus is to stop your brain from feeling out of control and bring yourself back to a healthier state. Because coping skills are a major part of promoting mental wellness, conquering coping skills is absolutely essential to rocking your teenage years.

What is Mental Illness?

Your teenage years are an incredibly important time for your social, physical, and emotional development, but all of this change can take a toll on your mental well-being. However, this is different than being diagnosed with a mental illness such as anxiety, depression, bipolar disorder, and more. While stress is a normal part of the human existence, mental illness is a medical diagnosis that typically needs to be treated with therapy or sometimes medication.

The most common mental illnesses that you will hear about are anxiety disorders; behavior disorders (such as attention deficit hyperactivity disorder, commonly known as ADHD);

eating disorders; and depression or mood disorders. Behavioral disorders can impact your education because they can make it difficult for you to concentrate, make you feel restless, or cause your mind wander in a way that makes it hard for you to focus on your work. Eating disorders, on the other hand, involve abnormal eating habits, extreme concern about your body weight, and an obsession with food. As for anxiety and depression, we'll go into those a little deeper in the sections below.

Depression

Depression is often associated with extreme sadness, but there are many other symptoms of depression. In fact, the most common symptom of depression in your teenage years is being withdrawn. Being withdrawn means that you stop doing the things that make you feel happy. Further, when you have depression, you might have changes in your appetite, have less energy, sleep more or less than usual, and struggle with school.

Depression is what we call an internalizing disorder, meaning that it mostly impacts your emotional well-being and the symptoms are often internal. Sometimes, other people may not even know how you are feeling inside. Depression can become serious when or if you start to have thoughts of suicide. However, if you feel worthless, guilty, or extremely fatigued for long periods of time, it may be worth it to seek help with your mental health.

Anxiety

Anxiety symptoms have to do with your body's fight-or-flight response. When you experience a stressful event, your body sends out hormones and undergoes a reaction that helps keep your body alert until you reach safety. With an anxiety disorder, those bodily systems are constantly keeping your body on high alert. This can lead to anxiety.

If you feel anxious, you might also feel restless, have trouble sleeping, withdraw from activities, feel irritable, and even start to experience body aches. Anxiety can be difficult to manage, but coping skills and other self-care strategies can help you deal with anxiety. But as with depression, if you feel anxious most of the time and have a hard time managing your emotions, it's worth it to talk to your parents, guardians, or your doctor.

Let's Talk About Coping Skills

Now that you know a bit about mental wellness and mental illness, we can start talking about ways to manage stress and hopefully learn how to cope with negative emotions. The thing about coping skills is that not every technique will work for every person. In fact, coping skills often are tied to your interests and hobbies.

For example, if you are really into art, coloring, or drawing, these activities may be a great way for you to channel your energy and attempt to block out negative emotions. If you are into exercising, running can be a great way to blow off some steam and feel a bit better about yourself. When it comes to establishing good coping mechanisms, you might have to try a couple out before you find what works.

There are a few different types of coping mechanisms. The first type of coping mechanism is problem focused. With problem-focused coping skills, the purpose of the strategy is to find practical ways to solve problems or reduce stress. For example, if your boss starts scheduling you for three shifts a week at your new job instead of two, you might need to have a conversation with them to figure out a better schedule or see if you can move your hours to the weekend if working during the week is too much. With this type of coping mechanism, you come up with a solution to help remove the stressor.

The next type of coping strategy is emotion focused. Emotion-focused coping skills are meant to help you manage the feelings that are caused by stressful events. For example, you might take a bath, go for a hike, or spend an evening reading your favorite book. These are all ways that you can focus on taking care of yourself instead of dwelling too much on the stressful event. Interested in getting more coping mechanism ideas? You can try these as well:

- Meditating
- Reading
- Talking to a friend or family member
- Gardening
- Listening to music
- Petting an animal
- Walking or hiking through nature
- Deep breathing
- Photography

- Journaling
- Physical activities

There is a difference between coping skills and self-care. Whereas coping skills are activities that can help you manage a stressful situation, self-care is something that you should do regardless of how stressed you are. Think of coping skills as a more reactive approach to stress, while self-care is something you should be doing regularly.

Unhealthy Coping Skills

Not all coping skills are healthy. If you deal with a lot of stress or have experienced trauma in your life, it can be all too easy to develop unhealthy coping skills that do you more harm than good. These coping skills can make us feel good despite also having some negative side effects.

One of the most common unhealthy coping mechanisms is simply avoiding things that make you feel uncomfortable. If something doesn't feel right, doesn't it make sense just to avoid it and run away? Well, if you do that, you'll never learn how to face that stressor or deal with it in the future. Plus, avoiding all negativity is impossible, and it will likely catch up with you eventually. Even though you may crave control in your life, sometimes you need to learn how to face stressors head on and work through them.

In some cases, alone time can be just what you need to recharge and feel good about yourself. Other times, isolation can be harmful. If you're going through a rough time and you continuously isolate yourself from people you care about, it might be harder to pick yourself up and move on. We do need other people to provide us with support, so make sure you have people around that you can go to when you need help.

Finally, the last common type of unhealthy coping mechanism is catastrophizing. Catastrophizing is when you mentally prepare for the worst possible situation or jump to conclusions that might be over the top. As a teenager, you might find yourself catastrophizing a lot, and this can make you worry more and feel worse about stressful situations.

For instance, you might overthink about what you said in a group chat or panic that the math quiz you bombed is going to destroy your grade. You might even feel like missing out on one social event will end the world. However, most of the time, you just need to think through some of these thoughts because they are often inaccurate. Try some problem-solving coping mechanisms instead.

It's Okay to Ask for Help

Although coping mechanisms are important to master and they can work in many stressful situations, sometimes you need to go to a professional for extra help. If you are feeling depressed or anxious, you might need to see a licensed therapist or counselor to help you better manage your mental well-being.

If you have ever thought of hurting yourself or experienced suicidal thoughts, talk to your parents, your doctor, or another trusted adult right away. These thoughts can be incredibly damaging, so the best thing you can do is get extra support. Asking for help is essential in these situations, and it might be what you need to help get your life back on track. If you think that you need professional help, talk to your parents or your school counselor to get more information.

CHAPTER 9:

THE TRUTH ABOUT SOCIAL MEDIA

Everyone spends a ton of time on their phone looking at social media. It doesn't matter if you're watching videos, liking pictures, or creating content of your own. Everyone seems to be glued to screens these days. Even though almost everyone is on social media, and it's likely something that you do in your free time, there are actually many negative effects of using social media.

This can seem odd because social media is such a normal part of everyone's lives. After all, if everyone uses it, how can it be bad? Well, one of the main issues with social media is that being online can skew reality.

The Negative Effects of Social Media

Maybe you are glued to your phone like everyone else, or maybe you have a fear of missing out, which is why you're always updating your feed. Maybe you just like to watch funny videos of cats. Regardless of what you like to do on your phone, there are still negative impacts of using social media.

When you scroll through your phone, you see pictures of family, friends, celebrities, and influencers that are targeted at you so that you continue to use the app. The internet is a dangerous place because technology can continue to recommend videos and pictures that you will likely enjoy. So, it's no wonder that you continuously scroll on your phone.

Poor Body Image

Photoshop is a real thing. Even though you may subconsciously know that the influencers who have perfect bodies don't always look perfect, it can be difficult to remember that when they post such amazing pictures. The problem is that those influencers probably took 100 pictures just to get that one, and they are posed so perfectly that it looks like they're flawless. Furthermore, they might even use filters and other types of digital-enhancement tools to make them look even "better."

But even though none of those pictures are truly real, it can still take a toll on your body image. When you see pictures of influencers and other people, you subconsciously begin to compare yourself to them. This can have negative effects on your emotions and make it difficult to distinguish the cyber world from reality. You might start to think negatively about your own body and hold yourself to unrealistic expectations of what you think you should look like.

Cyberbullying

Bullying became a problem long before social media came to light. However, cyberbullying is something unique to modern computers and phones. Cyberbullying is essentially bullying in the virtual world. Instead of being mean to your face, cyberbullies can post negative comments or material that's targeted toward you or another person.

In addition, the bullying can happen at any point. Cyberbullying can happen while you're at school, but it can also happen late at night and cause you significant distress when you should be resting.

You're Less Happy

Social media is actually linked to happiness, just not in the way you want it to be. In fact, the more you scroll, the less happy you're likely to be. With more use of social media, depression rates actually increase. In addition, there is a relationship between social media and poor mental health. Whether it's because you're constantly comparing yourself to unrealistic role models or experiencing cyberbullying, excessive use of social media definitely has an impact on your happiness.

Healthy Social Media Habits

Phones have become such an integral part of our lives that you can't be expected to completely swear off social media. However, there are several healthy habits you can do to make sure you're using social media in a healthy way. That said, try some of these tips for using your phone and browsing social media:

- Create your own boundaries and respect others' boundaries.
- Report bullying when it happens.
- Limit screen time when possible.
- Be mindful of tone and language.

CHAPTER 10:

SELF-ESTEEM AND BODY IMAGE

Your self-esteem is your belief in yourself. Self-esteem is not only learning to like yourself, but it's also being able to love, respect, and value yourself. When you have high self-esteem, you believe your ideas, opinions, and feelings matter. Further, you believe that you are capable of being the successful woman you're destined to become.

What it Means to Have High Self-Esteem

High self-esteem is essentially a frame of mind. With high self-esteem, you identify your strengths and learn to overcome challenges. In addition, high self-esteem allows you to deal with life's ups and downs so that you can come out on top. Finally, having high self-esteem is the basis of being able to gain perspective on the world and understand that some things are not within your control.

Having high self-esteem is incredibly important because it helps you better overcome stress, deal with anxiety, remain composed under pressure, and look at life through a realistic lens. With high self-esteem, you can tackle challenges more readily and overcome adversity.

What Can You Do to Improve Self-Esteem?

Although it may seem difficult at times, you can be in charge of your self-esteem. By focusing on the things you're good at, surrounding yourself with people who lift you up, and becoming your own cheerleader, you can improve your self-esteem.

Focus on What You Do Well

The first step in improving your self-esteem is focusing on your talents, skills, and what you do well. You already have so many things you can do well, so list those out! It doesn't matter how obscure your talents are; you should embrace them. Maybe you're an amazing opera singer, can say the entire alphabet backwards, or can hold your breath for more than a minute. These are all talents, and you should focus on them! Start listing out everything you're good at or even ask your friends and family about what they see as your best skills and talents.

Set Goals You Can Work Toward

Unrealistic goals will almost always end poorly. While you can reach almost any goal you set your mind to if you work hard, sometimes it's much easier to set smaller, attainable goals. We're not saying you should give up your dream of being the first person to live on Mars, but you should set goals that you're likely to achieve. These goals can all lead to one larger goal, but they should be something that you know you can do.

For example, if you're trying to become doctor, you should first focus on being successful in school. After that, you can think about taking Advanced Placement (AP) classes, applying to a good college, and getting accepted into a pre-med program. By establishing these smaller goals, you are also ultimately setting yourself up for success in achieving your larger goal.

Surround Yourself with People Who Lift You Up

Your friends, family, coworkers, and the people around you can be some of your greatest cheerleaders. However, there are some people who simply don't have your best interests at heart. Instead of surrounding yourself with the people who tear you down, judge you, or talk behind your back, hang out with the people who want to see you be successful. The best people to have around are the ones who will support you but also challenge you to do your best every day.

Work to Embrace Your Quirks

We all have some quirks that make us unique, so embrace yours and be unapologetically yourself! You should never have to pretend to be someone you're not or hide something about yourself just to fit in. Instead, figure out what makes you unique, and let the world know about it! It doesn't matter if you love anime, have an obsession with neon, or decide to travel the world before settling down — just make the choice to embrace yourself and be happy.

Focus on What You Can Change

There will always be things you can and cannot change. Rather than dwelling on the things you can't change, you need to focus on the things you can. If you focus on what you can control, such as the friends you choose to hang out with or your attitude toward something, then you will be a lot happier in the long run. If it helps, try making a list of everything you are worried about and categorize them in *can control* and *can't control* categories. That way, you can decide on what you want to target or change.

Use Self-Affirmations

Self-affirmations are little self-esteem boosters that you can tell yourself when you need an emotional boost. It doesn't matter if you put your affirmations on sticky notes on your mirror, repeat them to yourself when you get up in the morning, or write them down in your planner as long as they make you feel confident about yourself. For example, you could use these common affirmations:

- "I am strong."
- "I am confident."
- "I am enough."
- "I am fearless."
- "I am attracting positive vibes."
- "I am an amazing person."

Accept Compliments

Even though it should be the easiest thing you can do, accepting compliments can be incredibly difficult. When someone compliments you, whether it's on your new hair style, a new pair of shoes, the bright-red lipstick you wear, or how kind you treat those around you, learn to simply say "thank you" and accept that compliment! In fact, one of the first steps in raising your self-esteem is learning to accept compliments and discovering the amazing features that people appreciate about you.

Above All, Love Yourself!

Loving yourself and learning to accept all your quirks is cliché. However, it truly is the most important thing you can do to boost your self-esteem. You may hear this on repeat from social media, family, and friends, but you are your biggest critic. Whether you start by recognizing the little things or completely fall head over heels for your fabulous self, you can start your journey to promote full self-love.

CHAPTER 11:

HOW TO FIND THE PERFECT HIGH SCHOOL JOB

As a teenager, you might find yourself wanting to make money so that you can have more freedom, save up for a car, or put away money for college. Even if you just want a little extra "fun money" to spend with your friends, getting a job is one of your best options. Furthermore, jobs can be a great way to fill up your time and make a little extra cash.

How to Choose the Perfect Job

One of the trickiest parts of finding a job is finding the perfect one that fits with your schedule and interests. As a high schooler, you most likely need to find jobs that you can work on the weekends or the evenings. However, some students do take PSEO or college classes in high school, and they have a little more flexibility with their schedule. But if you're like most high school students, those weekend and evening gigs are the way to go.

Focus on Your Interests

You don't have to work a job you don't like. Instead, you will have a lot more fun when you can work a job that you enjoy. For example, if you like working with kids, you can try working for a local daycare. If you're interested in baking, you might want to try working at your local bakery or grocery store. Furthermore, you could even indulge your coffee addiction by working as a barista at a coffee shop. Regardless of your interests, try to find a job that sounds fun to you.

Full-Time vs. Part-Time

The difference between full-time and part-time work is in the name. Whereas full-time is considered 40 hours a week, part-time work can be anything from 5 hours a week to over 30. During the school year, it might be best to work part-time, but you may be able to work full-time in the summer depending on the law. Since you're still a kid, a part-time job should make you more than enough money to save and still have a little bit of fun.

The type of job that you take on will depend on your individual situation. You can make a choice determined by how much money you need and any legal limits to how many hours you can work because of your age.

Summer Job vs. Year Round

Some high schoolers choose to work summer-only jobs instead of having to work year round. In fact, there are many jobs out there that are only seasonal and can only be worked during the summer months. For example, you might work at a party company that focuses on putting up tents for events, or you could work at a theme park that is only open during the spring through fall months.

One of the benefits of working a summer job is that you don't have to work during the school year. That way, you can focus on your education without having to worry about going to work after school. However, many students can also work year round and just reduce their hours during the school year. If you're not in a ton of clubs or sports, you should absolutely be able to work a few hours during the school week to get a little extra money. Most of the time, employers will be very flexible and let you change the number of hours that you need depending on the time of year.

How to Get a Job as a Teenager

There are many ways to get a job as a teenager. From applying online to talking to the people you know and networking, the first step is to find out what's available. But before you get started, there are some things that you need to know about applying for jobs.

Build a Resume

A resume is a document that lists all your work experience and skills. Typically, your resume will have your name, contact information, professional experience, education, and skills. Resumes might also include any awards or honors that you have achieved, the courses that you've taken, and your hobbies or interests.

When you build a resume, you want to make sure that it's visually pleasing but also includes all required information. There are many resume templates that you can find online, so don't have to worry about having to format it yourself. While you want the resume to look good, you also should avoid making it too visually busy or overwhelming. It's best to avoid wild colors and excessive graphics.

Once you've built a resume, you're ready to start applying for jobs by submitting it online or handing it to store owners and managers who are hiring. Your resume will serve as a snapshot of yourself. It also tells interested parties how to contact you for an interview, so make sure to keep it updated.

Ask Your Family and Friends to See Who's Hiring

Networking can be one of the most important skills you'll need as you're hunting for a job. More often than not, your family and friends will know about people who are hiring. Plus, it looks really good to have someone refer you to a job because they can provide a personal recommendation and make sure your application ends up on the hiring manager's desk.

Apply to Jobs Online

There are many online platforms that serve as job boards where employers can post openings and prospective employees can submit their applications. This is quickly becoming the most common and popular way to apply to a job. While there are larger job websites such as Indeed or

LinkedIn, some companies also have their own application website. When you are looking to apply for a job, make sure you read the full job description to see how the company would like you to submit your application.

Ask for Applications in Person

If you live in a smaller town or you're applying to a smaller business, sometimes going into the store in person and asking for a physical application can be the way to go. Furthermore, some retail stores and restaurants have paper copies of their applications on site, so going in and physically filling out an application can make you stand out ahead of the crowd. Plus, you might get a chance to talk to current employees or managers. This will help them remember who you are and recognize your name when they see it later.

Helpful Tips for Interviewing

After you've submitted your application, you might be selected for an interview. The interview process is typically the next step in getting a job. Sometimes, the first interview could be over the phone with a recruiter who simply wants information about your availability and skill set. After that, you may make it to a second round of interviews with the hiring manager or the people you could be working with.

Interviews can be over the phone, virtual, or even in person. You should be ready for any type of format. Regardless of the intensity of the interview you are about to do, there are some helpful tips that you should know beforehand, such as:

- Dress to impress.
- Make eye contact.
- Hold your head up high, and walk with confidence.
- Avoid saying "um" too many times.
- Shake the interviewer's hand.
- Bring a copy of your resume.
- Do research so that you're prepared to explain why you chose to apply to that company.
- Research and understand the job description you are applying for so that you can talk about the specific responsibilities and skills you'll need.
- Send a thank-you email after the interview.
- Be yourself!

The Best Jobs for Teen Girls and High Schoolers

There are so many job opportunities for teenage girls and high schoolers. While it often depends on where you live, many states will allow you to start working some hours around the age of 14 or 15. However, many states do require you to be at least 16 before working more hours. Make sure you brush up on your state's employment laws before you start looking for jobs.

Once you're of age to start working, you should consider the most common jobs for teenage girls in high school. These jobs include but are not limited to:

- Lifeguard
- Coffee barista
- Fast food worker
- Dog walker and pet sitter
- Babysitter
- Retail sales associate
- Grocery store clerk

CHAPTER 12:

PREPARING FOR COLLEGE AND BEYOND

At the end of your teenage years, you will make one of the biggest decisions of your life: whether or not you want to go to college and what you would like to study if you choose to go. Your college years and major will help determine the job that you will get afterwards. It's never too early to prepare for college and beyond.

College Prep Can Start in Middle School

As a middle schooler, the best ways to start your college prep is to learn how to be the best student you can be. Start exploring career options, investigate colleges and the majors they offer, and talk to those around you to see you what you might be interested in.

Start Thinking About Your Future

Considering your future should include looking into which colleges you might be interested in attending. You should start to think about the potential areas that you might want to study so that you can narrow down your search over time. One of the best ways to do this is to share your thoughts and ideas with your family and friends at school.

Furthermore, teachers can be an awesome resource for discussing potential college and career ideas.

Your parents or guardians can absolutely help you research important parts of getting into college. This includes the types of classes you should take in high school and the activities or clubs that you should join to have a better chance of acceptance. For example, if you're interested in becoming a lawyer, you might want to look into joining the debate team. If you're interested in working with children, see if you can volunteer at a local daycare or after-school program.

Another awesome college-planning activity is talking to the adults in your life to see you what they do and don't like about their careers. You could talk to your teacher, school counselors, relatives, or other family friends who have jobs that interest you. You can ask them about the education that you would need to work in that career, what they like the best about their field, and any tips that they have for high school and college.

Ask Your Parents About a College Fund, and Start Saving

Sometimes, parents or guardians are able to put money away for your college fund. Although not everyone will have this privilege, it's a great place to begin when you're deciding how much money you need to save for college.

Even if you do have a college fund, you should start saving more if you haven't already. Although most students will work a job as they go through school, having some extra money from high school can serve as an excellent cushion so that you can focus more on your studies and less on having to work in college. You could even pay for your college classes out of pocket instead of having to rely on student loans.

Finally, don't worry if you are short on the funds for college. In fact, most students will take out student loans regardless of whether they have money saved up or a college fund. There are so many scholarship, grants, and loan programs that can help support you through college so that you can focus on your education and not have to worry about money until you have a job and you're out in the workforce.

Take Classes that Challenge and Interest You

Although you can absolutely take easier classes and get good grades in school, one way to become the best student you can is to take classes that challenge you. In fact, these challenging classes might end up being the classes that spark your love for a certain topic and ultimately influence your choice of college major. Try taking biology, chemistry, engineering, or other interesting classes that aren't just mainstream.

Learn How to Become a Good Student

The best way to become a good student is to learn how to manage your time, develop strong study skills, and organize your schedule. Studying and education are different experiences for everyone, so you may need some trial and error before you learn the time-management and organizational techniques that work for you. Some of the easy ways to get started include keeping a planner, trying not to procrastinate, and asking for help when you need it.

Volunteer and Become Involved in Your Community

Even in middle school, you can volunteer in your community to build up your community-service hours. Colleges often like to see students who are active in their community and taking the time to improve their environment. See if you can join some local organizations as a volunteer. You can pick up trash on the side of the road, volunteer at a local shelter, or staff community events.

College Prep in High School

In high school, college prep starts to get a little more serious. In middle school you're likely doing some exploring, but as a high schooler, the classes you take, the groups you become a part of, and your grades all matter. Plus, as you become a junior and senior in high school, not only will you need to research schools, but you'll also have to start applying to the colleges that you want to attend.

Be Involved in Clubs, Sports, and Volunteer Groups

Many colleges like to see that you are involved in clubs, sports, and volunteer groups. When you choose groups, the most important thing is that you choose sports or clubs that you're interested in. For instance, if you like music, then you can absolutely become a part of a traveling choir or show choir. If you like running, try joining the track or cross-country team.

Although it's tempting to simply be a member of a group, it looks even better if you're able to become a leader. More likely than not, leadership roles will not become available until you're at least a junior, but if you're a part of a group for all 4 years of high school, you'll likely have a better chance of landing a leadership role.

Make Connections with Your Teachers

When it's time to start applying for colleges, you will need to get letters of recommendation from your teachers. Instead of scrambling at the end and trying to find any teacher to write your letter of recommendation, make connections with your teachers early so that asking for a letter of recommendation is easier and less awkward.

To get to know your teachers, you can participate in class, ask questions, drop by during office hours, or make an appointment to talk about their classes.

Take Interesting Courses

Many colleges do require some courses to be admitted into their programs. All high schools will offer these courses, and your counselor should be knowledgeable about which ones you need to take. More likely than not, the required courses to graduate high school align exactly with what you need for college.

In addition to mandatory classes, make sure you also take ones that interest you. Many high schools offer the opportunity to take classes within various subjects and disciplines. You just might discover your passion by taking a class you never thought you'd be interested in.

Think About Potential Careers and Colleges

As you get closer to college, you should start to think more about potential careers. While some students will know exactly what they want to do in college, many students don't, and that is perfectly okay! It can be helpful to know the general area that you're interested in, but many students do go to college without a defined major.

If you already have a specific interest, research colleges that have strong programs in that area. For instance, you might look for a nursing school if you're interested in a medical career or colleges that offer strong pre-law programs if you intend to become a lawyer. You can even look for colleges that have a specific marine-biology program if you're set on becoming a dolphin trainer.

Visit College Campuses, Talk to Recruiters, and Meet with Current Students

Oftentimes, you will start to visit college campuses, talk to recruiters, and get to know some of your top colleges as a junior in high school. In fact, the best way to learn more about colleges is to visit them. You can take campus tours, set a time to talk to current students, or meet coaches if you're an athlete who intends to play in college.

Determine if You Need Standardized Test Scores

Many schools require college applicants to submit SAT or ACT test scores. However, not all schools require standardized tests, so make sure you do your research and figure out if you need to sign up or not. If a school does require standardized tests, they will often accept either the SAT or ACT. It usually doesn't matter which one you take, but check to be sure.

Research Scholarships

Scholarships are an excellent way to get money for school that you don't have to pay back. As a high schooler, you can start to apply for scholarships online or look to see if the schools you are interested in offer scholarship programs. You can also talk to college recruiters and campus counselors to see if they have any scholarship options that you qualify for.

Watch Out for the Senior Slide

The senior side is real. During your senior year, some students start to feel a little burned out and may not take their education as seriously. If you've already been admitted to a college and don't have to worry about applying, it can be all too easy to start letting some of your homework or studying slip.

If you can, avoid the senior slide. While you may feel like you're done after you get accepted, colleges do require you to maintain good grades during your last semester. Failing classes can compromise your admission status.

College Applications

When it's time to fill out college applications, it's important to know all of the pieces that go into one. While some schools will have their very own personalized application to fill out, you can also use The Common Application (Common App for short) to apply. The Common App is great because it will save all your information and make applying to colleges a lot easier. That way, you can submit applications to multiple colleges without having to upload your materials every time.

What Do You Need to Submit a College Application?

Luckily, many colleges require the same materials for all applications. Primarily, these application materials include:

- College essay where you have to answer a prompt or explain why you want to be admitted to that college

- Your personal information, such as data about yourself, your school, and your family
- High school transcripts so that schools know which classes you took and what your grades are
- Standardized test scores such as the SAT or ACT
- At least two letters of recommendation from your teachers but sometimes more

When Do You Submit a College Application?

College applications often open up in the fall, and the first deadlines are usually in early November. The November deadlines are typically the early-decision deadlines where you will hear back from a college sooner than those who turn in their applications later. Most colleges have application deadlines that go well into December and even January.

While early-decision applicants will usually hear back first, you will likely receive answers from colleges from mid-March through even early April. After you hear back, you typically have until around May 1 to decide which school you want to attend.

CONCLUSION

Congratulations! Now that you've finished this book and read through our top picks for surviving your teenage years, you're ready to take on the world and become the wonderfully authentic person that you're meant to be. As you go through life and experience various trials and tribulations, make sure you refer back to this book for any questions you may have about health, nutrition, relationships, puberty, and mental health.

Your teenage years will be filled with so many amazing experiences, and now you can enjoy them without having to worry about coming across situations that you're unsure about. That said, we will now release you into the wilderness of your up-and-coming teenage years. Best of luck, and always remember to be yourself!

Printed in Great Britain
by Amazon

13088919R00077